I0213791

Beast of the World

Poems

by

Chris Morgan

Finishing Line Press
Georgetown, Kentucky

Beast of the World

To Aidan

Will any come back will one

Saying yes

Saying look carefully yes
We will meet again

W.S. Merwin, "The Animals"

Copyright © 2023 by Chris Morgan
ISBN 979-8-88838-243-1 First Edition
All rights reserved under International and Pan-American Copyright Conventions.
No part of this book may be reproduced in any manner whatsoever without written
permission from the publisher, except in the case of brief quotations embodied in
critical articles and reviews.

Publisher: Leah Huete de Maines
Editor: Christen Kincaid
Cover Art: Ted Morgan and John Morgan
Author Photo: Chris Morgan
Cover Design: Elizabeth Maines McCleavy

Order online: www.finishinglinepress.com
also available on amazon.com

Author inquiries and mail orders:
Finishing Line Press
PO Box 1626
Georgetown, Kentucky 40324
USA

Table of Contents

Apertures

I

Snagged down
in marsh stars
bright as he was lead
he knew he no longer believed
in the reversals. A certain
slowing down perhaps but even
that a promise dirty as a rootless tree.
Not a real thing.
Not alive.
Merely a bandage over
eyes for fear
one might
be blind.

II

We tore the leaves out of the last trees.

Two by two we delivered the animals
into the burning world unaware

their fate lived inside us.
We ourselves are the fire

we said, foundering
over petroleum seas.

Two by two we sent them
away from us. One by one

we blew out the defoliate stars.
As ever, preferring the bred-to comfort

of extinguished light.

III

Darkness came
and we knew it was
coming since the darkness
was us.

Nonetheless
surprising the way darkness
works—the knowing inside
unknowing.

Its face
a stranger's

looming over
a mirror hiding

the old
unconcealable truths.

IV

More ashes, more burning—
the gathering autumn.

The narrowing aperture dusk.

What I must not do
I do and what is too far

must find ingress now.

Requires this precise lattice-
work of feathers over-

lapping into wings

light enough
to make a ladder

of air.

V

My journey was staying here.
My song was immense silence.
My dance merely a stillness as
I waited in gaps widening
from the inside out
and breathed.
Only this,
palms up.

Not backing off the hunger.
Never finishing with thirst.

Zeteki

One day I will go to Varanasi to die.
Not yet though; I'm too busy with love.

Over the phone to El Valle
I can hear the rain hushing the forest,

falling in the rushing stream
at his lush feet in their rubber boots.

I too am hunting the Golden Frog.
We are searching together, apart.

He in the high jungle streams;
me mundane at a sea-level desk.

From this remove when the satellites fail
we resort to semaphore signals,

waving across a continent and the sea
between, as if there might be sides.

As if there were such a thing as extinction.
As if death didn't turn us to gold.

Satao

Do not forgive us
the last unforgivable desecration.
There will be others you know,
as we close on the end.

When we brought you to your knees
with a poisoned dart at the watering hole
it was ourselves kneeling before you
God of Ivory—the crippled race,
Insatiable Man.

When we hacked off your face
and carried it away with us to be sold
for the trinkets of Asia it was to make you
faceless as ourselves.

You must understand this once
and for all your extinguished kind:

What we have desired we have always killed.

In the Age of Blood your forgiveness,
Gentle Master, is irrelevant.

Aeschylus at Home

With the rivers all on fire
migrations blocked by meltwater
pipelines like ceaseless elongations
of the phallus of the mind of man
what are we to do but kneel down
before the apocalypse into hands
thorned with tears?
                    Among the demagogues
the armies the poets at a loss for words
anymore there is nothing but the effete
cry no word left for the nameless loss
and longing only the ancient tropes
sackcloth and ashes rending of hair
putting out the eyes for regret.

Frost Warning

What you have become
to me is a shocking loveliness
glimpsed and gone; glimpsed again.
Like fern-life in half-light.
Summer-peach. Dawn-sea.
A thing dark and deep as woods
I peered into once from a meadow's
bright edge, aching to cross over,
waiting in the aching.

How have I resisted
the invitation of your trees,
your deep shade and bird-song,
promise of your pebble-bottomed streams
clear enough to sip?

Shock of Love: forgive me
thirst and hesitation. Forgive me
ardor, avidity, the running away.
Forgive the stubborn, shattered heart.
And how I have become all frost—
the promises, the miles, no sleep in sight.

A Thin Place

Marsh grass whispers
he is here since he returned
trailing the smoke of jungles,
bat wings, moss-damp
of vines in his webbed hair.
I sit wondering if howler
monkeys still boom savagely
in his untamed ears, rhythms
of thatch spill the memory
of his hands. What of the
comfortable impress at his
waist where the clasp-knife
no longer waits for its work
in cane, snapper, guayaba?

No deadly snakes inhabit
this windowed place where
he rests in a sleep full of the
music of rain falling on a thin
country, people he loved there
that live inside him now, he
in them. Is his rest deaf to songs
of grass, to this ocean mouthing
his name in waves?

But I hear them.
Clear as I hear his quiet
breathing in the room upstairs.
Even so busy as I am these days,
practicing the holding on,
practicing the letting go.

eremocene

god of love where are you?
we cry but our gadgets fail
to transmit the dull song
of longing through atmospheres
irradiated by unfiltered light
the sloughed oceans impenetrably
tangled in sonar news of an enemy
plot we wail on indecipherably
raw with hubris and despair
at the vast dark between stars
beaching on the littered shores
plastiglomerate deserts god
no longer visits for fear

Standings

1.

Nonetheless an onlooker
I did not elect to come
for this death.
Obligation not love
bore me like a lost uncle
to phlegm-rattle of the last breath.

Nothing to do now but turn
from this slum bay,
nitrogen saturated, phosphorous rich:
not the dark energy of space
but dead zone of human waste.

2.

The brown-eyed dog
whose yellow light reminds
noses the raped shore.

I came for this,
not with Byron shouting for the dance.

I have dressed in black.
I wear the ashes of earth in my hair.
Let despair have her way
with the triumph of my kind.
I sing in my day of unmendable gaps.
Softly under the din of cities,
their minions worshipping the satellite gods,
I whistle my dirge where her body
lies in state, voluptuous even in death.

3.

We created it, they cry, *from our flesh!*
Instantly its messages squall
over the world, the new weather of Love.

We repeat in sacred unison our Apostles Creed.
At ten million altars we worship nightly
the shifting glow of its savior-face
that is always different and forever the same,
its presence a deepening numbness in the veins.
Gratefully we enter the stagnant rapture of its void.
On distended tongues our children take the Eucharistic coin.

4.

Look what we have made! I cry,
sweeping my pale arms over the cities of earth,
raising my arms above the ashen land.

My conviction astounds even me.

As over infidels I shout them down,
articulate for their conversion
the necessity of expanding economies.
Into the graveyard of the sea I pour
my words (this liberty, this equality, this fraternity)
while somewhere down deep and quietly
the bones of whales turn over amidst
raw litter of the world.

species counterpoint

i

reflections off
the still creek play
up through branches
of autumn poplars
on the bank
i am there
too silent witness
stripped to the waist
a river behind me
as felted hammers
slip over woody
resonators chiming
my bells of light

ii

if i listen carefully
to the dinning of the Machine
that eats itself through days and nights
but is never not ravenous
i sometimes catch the undersong
of earth soft as a chorus of wrens
and the grief that i have called
poor names becomes suddenly accountable,
becomes my own grief

catadromous

if they could have paused
a moment they might have
recognized the furious tumult
of their age was nothing (and
everything) but the amalgamated
yearning for gods the webbed
undertow of an ocean that
once bore them earthward
calling them back to the equal
acceleration of zero gravity
greater silence of the deep

Bubo Scandiacus

The winter he turned fifty
owls ranged out of Canada
farther south than ever before,
trajectories driven by hunger
in the year without lemmings.

Mostly they preferred coastal
dunes they imagined as loose
translations of arctic tundra.
Hook-nosed and lemon-eyed
they ghosted the frozen beaches
of Rhode Island, meditated
on factory awnings in PA.
There was report of an ivory
stole, charcoal-flecked, bloodied
by dolphin entrails and dangling
a smashed wing amongst the wrack
of a Chincoteague nor'easter.

Brooklyn, Arkansas, Florida even.
Elusive and incarnational as news of God.

He knew he was one
of them—solitary diurnal
ravenous in a place that
could no longer provide.

In the darkest days that year
with bitter winter descending
he watched the weak sun round
on a low line and understood
whatever life remained lay out
beyond him now, an unknown
into which he must trust and plunge,
winged raptor, exile starving
in a world rare with blood.

September

A missionary urgency
increasing in its frequency
the knock-knocking went.

My head in the clumped trowel of the pen,
furrows of the late garden of the page.
My head an amnesia of light.

That evening cooler than I couldn't
remember, darker earlier under
the little shatter of a leaf.

I pulled the shut door wide on its dried stem
to discover a dishevelment of hay-yellow hair,
feet scuffed by what's become of time.

Berry lips,
rose hips,
eyelet velvet as chestnut rind.

I recognized her pale radiance: an old flame
returned like a dim-down sun to my summer arms,
luscious and low-slung and sexed for the harvest dusk.

Conspiracy Theory

It was late
one of December's last gasping
nights

the year dying
out of itself in breaths measured
in ice

and geese high
up somewhere on the low-slung plateau
of cloud

I could not
see I could only hear their muscular
calling

back and forth
one to another until I began to imagine
them

working
together in grey blindness of winter
a unity

in the
undefeated conspiracy of life
to live

and I
yearned to be journeying in my own
urgent skein

and I
desired the wild brotherhood resembling
prayer

to spend
my breath calling across waste darkness
gathering

replies
understanding over and over how I was
not alone

Llueve!

Something deeply theological
was about to happen. You could feel
it in the marbled thunder, soft
and far as possibility.
There came a sudden shush
of birds, stilled wind. The sky dropped,
bruised, blotting itself plum
against a high ridge in the north.

We'd been thirsty so long
by then. Since November, they said.
The forest was dead-tired, a pallid
corpse in its dusty shroud.

When it happened the men ran
into the dry bones of the road with their arms
wide and palms turned, their heads angled
heavenward like criminals granted mercy
following the long siege of shame.

I can hear their whoops.
The cries as first droplets pucker
and fall, line the dark country
of their faces like tears squeezed
from the heart's drought. I watch
the soft joy of the women watching.
See the trees shiver, their livid skins
slicked with diamonds in the sudden
cleft of electric light.

Pine

Not the tree
that sang outside my window
in New Hampshire the winter
I was twenty-one
and in love and would lie
awake after she'd gone, listening
in the darkness with the taste
of her in my mouth.

Not the Carolina pine either,
its summer bed cool under my naked
feet where I stooped to peer at the sea,
its horses running, their cylindrical manes.

No, the verb.
What my heart practices
in its emptiness. Calling out
to itself and waiting—
but no answer comes,
not even an echo.

Thief

Should I? he asked.
Not yet, she said.
She said it quietly
through breathing,
her face above him
in the darkness rising
and falling, Venus
in zodiacal light.

Later they ate tomatoes
stolen from the neighbor's
garden. Diced in oil and salt.
Cold from the refrigerator.

Ate them in the warm dark
as summer ran out of itself
just like a blue thread
off the spool.

Anoxia

He went missing in October.
There was a photo of a red dirt road
through the front window of a bus
in which you could make out meadow
hay in the grey light, the basal rosettes
of sea lavender, slender glasswort,
vast flats of black needlerush.

His sister sent an urgent note:
where are you and what are you doing?

They all knew about the dog.
His legs trailing uselessly in the end,
spindle ropes and the bloodied knuckles
on top where the delicate fur used to be.

How he carried the dog
like a paraplegic lover. In and out
of the shackled house to move his bowels
lying down in the burned grass.

How they slept together, the big retriever
on his chest where they could feel each other's breath.
Then put him down in the evening woods,
watching as the eyes dimmed back
in leave-taking to another side.

It was Thanksgiving when they found him.
Not in the salt pannes of the tide-islands
where they'd searched but far inland.
Deep in the Monongahela. Fasting,
climbing. Watery eyes luminous
with belonging to earth.

Lullaby

Where have you gone my Sika, my dear?
Dancing on marsh under the windy moon.

> *Glasswort is salt,*
> *needlerush nut.*

My speckled, my tide-island deer,
where are you now in the sweep and thrum?

Singing, singing:

> *Sedges have edges,*
> *rushes are round.*

With the egrets all flown away whitely.
With the dark at the end of your days.

Sweetly a song by the shore,
lavender snow in your hair:

> *Sedges have edges*
> *and rushes are round,*
> *grasses are flat from*
> *their tips to the ground.*

Perennials

One day the heart hiccups,
but not with love.

Later they put his ashes
in a cedar box with a brass plaque
on the front and I buried it
between the pear trees
where he lay summers
in the dapple shade
watching the birds.

Watching me writing when
he thought I couldn't see.

Please to stand up
when the world comes
for you dressed in its black
crepe de chine.

Smile.
Look into its lamed eyes.
Say how once you lived.

It's funny how one death gathers
the others up from slumber.

From a single flower blooms
a fire-colored field of grief—
dazzling, new all over.

Like a Death Valley superbloom.
Or like the synchronicity of corals.

Just like that the cryptochrome
proteins Cry1 and Cry2 open their eyes
to blue light, melt the azoic heart.

Spending the Light

Some people never grow up.

Thinking that sentence, racing
the November light, the light-tackle
spin-rod tilting over my left handlebar
like Don Q's lance charging
the windmill dusk.

I'd spent most of the afternoon
paddling Watson Creek until
my fingers were a blistered mess.
Catching the last trees dressed
in their colors, buffing the banks
on either side. Geese overhead.
Late osprey longing for second homes
in Ecuador. And the stripers raging
under my feet. I could feel them—
the suck and thrum, their flexions
rapacious as sea-wolves sensing
the clench of a first freeze.

There are moments one suspects
the wilderness of God's mind—an imagination
never tethered to begin with, possibly run amok.
The same as mine pedaling against time
and light, pen in hand, leaving so much
undone in my wake to pursue *maybe*
and *might*. Sacrificing everything
for this mandatory attention
to the heart's need.

How You'll Know

How will you ever know yourself
if you've never paddled a canoe home
in moonless December dark, your arms
aching with the day's hunt, your slow
breath blowing in ghosts, geese barking
but invisible when you look up?
How without frenzied fish crashing
your lures? How minus the sharpening
hunger and cold, the water rippling out
like a small voice from paddle and hull?
How will you ever know without the barren
tress becoming a darkness pouring on either side
of the river and when you get there the creek
in black silk, the few houses on either side lit
for Christmas? And not one sound but the water
moving and once the beating of a heron's
wings close by? How without all that
will your heart become a flame
against the shortening of days?

Asking the Geese

Do bluefish nibble your rubber feet?

Who taught you aerodynamics of long-flight
slipstreams in the rotating V-formation?

Or to steer the burnished flyways of your kind?

And the honking.
Where does it come from?
Is it society, reassurance merely?
Or the caught-out notes of a song
of longing for fecund earth?

Is it true, autumn is only
a beginning? That far places
anticipate our arrival? If only
we lift our wings over the desert
sea? Trust the invisible light?

Christmas

A child opened
its shriveled arms
to behold for the first time
the darkness through which kings
were travelling, fording
the deserts of their own hearts
in search of a rumor before
which they could pour whatever
might be left of themselves
like wine or blood over
the raging sand.

(M)other Tongue

Nameless one not yet, I said.
*Who will speak for the animals
in their silence that we no longer
understand?*
                              Like the three
deer in the meadow, ghostly
at dusk. Close enough
I can hear their breathing,
the soft munching in half-light,
quarter-light, lost to sight
in the dropped dark.
                              After-song
of their thin legs tinkling
marsh water is the language
I want to speak.

Praying to the Gods

Gazing through river birch
at the half-lantern of the faded moon
in a grey-glass sky I begged
the gods in grief:

strike lightning,
send rain,
set me burning
in a world aflood
with afterwards a dove.

I imagined the devastating
plank-walk to safety
of the animals in their pain,
the last of them a second
time beginning again.

No answer: the river's tongue
mute in the river's mouth,
white-throated birch
in a wordless stand.

Merely a dwindling moon
in a verdigris sky,
planetary stillness-in-motion
of the gods receding
faster than light.

Song of Asking

Look into my eyes, love.
Imagine yourself into what I've seen:
the human cruelty, mad blather of a race,
plagues and the burning earth.

Love, touch my eyes
untouched now for a thousand years,
the quivering parchment
lids of all we've lost:
shapes of animals, webs of trees,
the blood-blue spilling rivers of light.

Kiss my eyes, love.
Open your lips like first spring
before the silence of birds.
Kiss my eyes in the waterless desert
as if we were children again
in unblemished wonder, before grief
taught the body knowledge
it was not made for time.

in my country

the masses rush
out into the light
created by money

we have! they cry
grasping after receding stars

as the poets huddle
in their beloved dark
celebrating being lost

with the gnashing of teeth
the rending of ashen hair

refugees turning fields
barren of everything
but grief

foxwise

separate from surmise
he sits with thorned eyes
inside a circle of late-summer

trees, a red whit wind-drifted
from anonymous woods,
slender-legged as a girl bundled
in a flame fur, scantling

sent to inherit the burning earth

as a gift he gives
no meaning—innocent
to thrall and compassionless
as in shackles made of money
i serve my sentences to time

his vanishing
completes the voiding world,
its loneliness of unknowing
who i am

or how to be free, how to give
thanks amidst the blood-gulping,
the quenchless race

Thumos

Heat destroying and lovely
the wind arrived like beauty and a knife.

We took turns making love,
working slowly with rough hands.

I woke grateful in birdsong, twined
about the warm coil of your absence.

It was the kind of dream one lingers in.

I wanted to push through thick undergrowth
of sleep to find you again.

Instead I went downstairs in the fetal light.
With spent hands prepared the meal:

touched the warm bread of your flesh,
raised the wild berry of your mouth to mine.

August

I came for the red oleander
on the forest road where once
I saw a girl on a white bicycle
with around her the sound of wind
or the sea I could not be sure
and when I looked again
through that dappled light
breaking over shoals of pine
she was gone I could not be
sure she was except the flower
of her mouth like a red
memory among the trees

Agon

I lived in the time
of the final desecration
of the temples of earth.

Which side in the agon was mine?

What finger did I lift
against rapacity of the monster race?

Is the fact that I'm alive a testament
to complicity, guilt?

Was I ever once a voice crying
in the wilderness of bone?

One by one the emperor trees
fell to the blades of new gods.

The sludged meadows glowed a moment
before withdrawing into ash.

Migrations blundered in petroleum seas.

I lived in that time.
I was a man of the Machine.
My little silence blessed the slaughter
of the elders of the world.

autobiography

they called me
to stand in late—sad piper,
just the man for the job

play something
for grief, they said

i blew my slow dirge over
the crumpled body
of earth

there was nothing to hear

Chris Morgan's stories have won the Sherwood Anderson Prize and the K. Margaret Grossman Award and been selected for inclusion the *Tulip Tree Stories That Need to Be Told* Anthology and the *Nowhere Magazine* Best Writing Print Annual. His work has been published in various literary journals and magazines in the US and abroad, among them *Mid-American Review, Literal Latte, North Carolina Literary Review,* and *Red Wheelbarrow*. He is the author of the book *R.S. Thomas,* a critical exploration of the life and work of the Welsh modernist poet. He recently completed work on a collection of short fiction titled, *Everywhere the Water*. He holds graduate degrees from St. John's College, Johns Hopkins University, and Aberystwyth University, Wales. *Beast of the World* is his first poetry chapbook. For more about his writing you can visit his website at *www.jchristophermorgan.com*.

www.ingramcontent.com/pod-product-compliance
Lightning Source LLC
Chambersburg PA
CBHW030459100426
42813CB00002B/283

9798888382431